Ulysses S. Grant

Military Leader and President

Colonial Leaders

Lord Baltimore
English Politician and Colonist

Benjamin Banneker
American Mathematician and Astronomer

Sir William Berkeley
Governor of Virginia

William Bradford
Governor of Plymouth Colony

Jonathan Edwards
Colonial Religious Leader

Benjamin Franklin
American Statesman, Scientist, and Writer

Anne Hutchinson
Religious Leader

Cotton Mather
Author, Clergyman, and Scholar

Increase Mather
Clergyman and Scholar

James Oglethorpe
Humanitarian and Soldier

William Penn
Founder of Democracy

Sir Walter Raleigh
English Explorer and Author

Caesar Rodney
American Patriot

John Smith
English Explorer and Colonist

Miles Standish
Plymouth Colony Leader

Peter Stuyvesant
Dutch Military Leader

George Whitefield
Clergyman and Scholar

Roger Williams
Founder of Rhode Island

John Winthrop
Politician and Statesman

John Peter Zenger
Free Press Advocate

Revolutionary War Leaders

John Adams
Second U.S. President

Ethan Allen
Revolutionary Hero

Benedict Arnold
Traitor to the Cause

King George III
English Monarch

Nathanael Greene
Military Leader

Nathan Hale
Revolutionary Hero

Alexander Hamilton
First U.S. Secretary of the Treasury

John Hancock
President of the Continental Congress

Patrick Henry
American Statesman and Speaker

John Jay
First Chief Justice of the Supreme Court

Thomas Jefferson
Author of the Declaration of Independence

John Paul Jones
Father of the U.S. Navy

Lafayette
French Freedom Fighter

James Madison
Father of the Constitution

Francis Marion
The Swamp Fox

James Monroe
American Statesman

Thomas Paine
Political Writer

Paul Revere
American Patriot

Betsy Ross
American Patriot

George Washington
First U.S. President

Famous Figures of the Civil War Era

Jefferson Davis
Confederate President

Frederick Douglass
Abolitionist and Author

Ulysses S. Grant
Military Leader and President

Stonewall Jackson
Confederate General

Robert E. Lee
Confederate General

Abraham Lincoln
Civil War President

William Sherman
Union General

Harriet Beecher Stowe
Author of Uncle Tom's Cabin

Sojourner Truth
Abolitionist, Suffragist, and Preacher

Harriet Tubman
Leader of the Underground Railroad

Ulysses S. Grant

Military Leader and President

Tim O'Shei

Arthur M. Schlesinger, jr.
Senior Consulting Editor

Chelsea House Publishers

Philadelphia

Dedication: To the Writing Club: Caitlin, Erin, Michelle, Katie, Jessica & Chris. Thank you!

Produced by 21st Century Publishing and Communications, Inc. New York, NY. http://www.21cpc.com

CHELSEA HOUSE PUBLISHERS
Production Manager Pamela Loos
Art Director Sara Davis
Director of Photography Judy L. Hasday
Managing Editor James D. Gallagher
Senior Production Editor J. Christopher Higgins

Staff for *ULYSSES S. GRANT*
Project Editor Anne Hill
Associate Art Director Takeshi Takahashi
Series Design Keith Trego

The Chelsea House World Wide Web address is
http://www.chelseahouse.com

First Printing
1 3 5 7 9 8 6 4 2

Library of Congress Cataloging-in-Publication Data

O'Shei, Tim.
    Ulysses S. Grant / Tim O'Shei.
      p. cm. — (Famous figures of the Civil War era)
    Includes bibliographical references (p.) and index.
    Summary: A biography of Ulysses Grant, from his childhood in Ohio, through his education at West Point and his career as an Army officer, to his terms as president of the United States.
    ISBN 0-7910-6001-2 (HC) — ISBN 0-7910-6139-6 (pbk.)
    1. Grant, Ulysses S. (Ulysses Simpson), 1822-1885—Juvenile literature. 2. Presidents—United States—Biography—Juvenile literature. 3. Generals—United States—Biography—Juvenile literature. 4. United States. Army—Biography—Juvenile literature. [1. Grant, Ulysses S. (Ulysses Simpson), 1822-1885. 2. Presidents. 3. Generals.] I. Title. II. Series.

E672.O84 2000
973.8'2'092—dc21
[B]
                             00-038393
                                 CIP

Publisher's Note: In Colonial, Revolutionary War, and Civil War Era America, there were no standard rules for spelling, punctuation, capitalization, or grammar. Some of the quotations that appear in the Colonial Leaders, Revolutionary War Leaders, and Famous Figures of the Civil War Era series come from original documents and letters written during this time in history. Original quotations reflect writing inconsistencies of the period.

30652000990612

Contents

Ulysses Grant helped out in the fields and around the farm. He was a shy boy who loved nature but didn't have many friends. Few people who knew him then could have guessed he would grow up to be president.

The Boy They Called "Useless"

seless. That's what the other boys called Ulysses Grant. Many didn't like him, didn't play with him, and didn't even talk to him. Small, freckle-faced, and terribly shy, Ulysses was a loner. Growing up in Georgetown, Ohio, he didn't have many friends. Kids his age picked on him and gave him that embarrassing nickname: Useless Ulysses. Nobody except his father, Jesse, thought he'd ever become someone special.

Those kids were wrong. "Lyss," who was named after the Greek hero Ulysses, was anything but useless. He would grow up to become one of America's greatest heroes. People would love him for winning the Civil War and saving the country. By the end of his life, Ulysses would be called many names, mostly "General Grant" or "Mr. President." But "Useless" was not one of them.

Born on April 27, 1822, Hiram Ulysses Grant was the oldest son in his family of three boys and three girls. He never dreamed of growing up to be a famous war general or a politician. Presidents usually enjoyed shaking hands and making speeches, but Ulysses was quiet. In fact, many years later as president, he once stood up to announce to a crowd that he had nothing to say.

Ulysses also didn't like violence. He grew sick at the sight of blood. His father owned a **tannery** across the road from the family home. Ulysses did anything he could to avoid working there. He hated being around the bloody animal **hides**. But he liked farming, so he helped out by hauling crops in the fields. The boy hoped to someday become either a farmer, a river trader, or a college-educated man.

When Ulysses was two, a neighbor decided to shoot a shotgun right next to his tiny head. The man was looking for some fun. He expected Ulysses to cry in terror. BANG! When the shot rang loud, Ulysses squealed in delight and reached out for the gun. But the toddler never heard well out of that ear again. People sometimes teased Ulysses about his bad hearing.

As Ulysses grew older, he disliked hunting. Even when he was in the army years later and was instructed to hunt animals for food, Ulysses couldn't bring himself to shoot an animal.

Nature was one of Ulysses' favorite things. Horses were probably his best friends. Ulysses'

It's not very surprising that Ulysses didn't want to be a tanner like his father. Making leather was difficult and dirty work. First you needed the skin, or "hide," of a dead animal, which was soaked in a chemical mixture made with lime. Then the skin was scraped free of all flesh and fur and soaked for a long time in both sulfuric acid and **tannic acid**. Several months after being placed in the goopy tannic acid, the skin was removed and washed thoroughly. The result was a "tanned hide," or leather.

parents thought their oldest son got along better with horses than people. When he was three, he liked to swing back and forth underneath a horse by its tail. Soon, his tricks grew more exciting. By age five, Ulysses could ride on the back of a horse like a circus showman.

Every year when the circus came to Georgetown, Ulysses would go. He knew that sometime during the show the ringmaster would step to the crowd and ask, "Will any boy come forth to ride this pony?"

The first time Ulysses heard the offer, another boy went first. Riding a squirmy, nervous pony is like trying to ride a roller coaster without a seat belt. The boy fell face-first into the sawdust while the crowd laughed.

Not at all scared, Ulysses volunteered next. Just five years old, he climbed onto the pony and rode smoothly around the ring. The excited crowd roared. For a few more years, Ulysses always volunteered to ride the circus pony. He put on a fine show each time.

Once a clown threw a monkey high into the air while Ulysses was riding. The screeching animal landed smack on the boy's head. With tiny monkey claws clinging to his hair, Ulysses continued his smooth ride.

By the time he was eight, Ulysses was so in love with horses that he badly wanted one of his own. His neighbor was selling one and wanted $25 for it. Ulysses went to his dad and asked for the money. Jesse thought the price was too high, but Ulysses begged and begged. Eventually Jesse gave in. He told Ulysses that he could offer the man $20. Jesse said that if that much money wasn't enough, the boy should raise the offer to $22.50. If that still was not enough, then Ulysses could give the man $25.

Delighted, Ulysses went to the man and reported, "Papa says I may offer you twenty dollars, but if you won't take that, I am to offer you twenty-two and a half, and if you won't take that, to give you twenty-five."

Ulysses got the horse for $25, of course. He

was pleased. Jesse wasn't. The other boys in town were amused by Ulysses' bad bargain and picked on him more: "Useless Ulysses."

Despite the bad deal, Ulysses' parents encouraged the boy to keep working with horses. Fearless and calm, Ulysses was talented at taming wild horses. When he was only nine years old, Ulysses was well-known among the townspeople as a master horseman. When they saw him riding through the center of town, they often said things like, "There's that boy Ulysses breaking in another horse." Once, Ulysses traded for a rough horse nobody wanted. He was confident he could tame the horse–and he did.

By the time Ulysses turned 10, his father had added a **livery** business to his tannery. Customers came from other parts of Ohio, and Ulysses helped out by driving them back and forth by horse and buggy.

Even though the 50-mile trip to a city like Cincinnati would take all day, it was fun for Ulysses. He would check into a hotel at night, then

Even as a boy, Ulysses was an excellent horseman. He loved to be around horses and worked hard in his father's stable.

explore the city the next morning and try to find somebody who needed a ride back home. The boy was young, but people trusted him. Ulysses once promised two ladies that he'd get them across a flooding river safe and dry, and he did.

Horses were Ulysses' love, but he didn't like it so much when his father tricked him into cleaning the smelly stables. Jesse took the boy to the stables and offered him a silver dollar if he could clean it with a shovel. Working hard, Ulysses managed to do it. He showed his father the clean stable and proudly accepted the silver dollar.

"You did it splendidly," Jesse told Ulysses, "and now I find you can do it so nicely, I shall have you do it every morning all winter."

Even though Ulysses' parents made him work hard, they also gave him time to have fun. He liked fishing, ice skating, and riding around on a horse and sleigh. An adventurous boy, Ulysses liked to stay active. But he didn't play a lot of games with other children, probably because of his shyness.

Ulysses had a few friends at school, but he didn't spend much time in classes. School only lasted for 13 weeks each winter. Ulysses spent the rest of the year working on the farm or doing something with horses. Jesse had taught his son to read at a very young age. Because very few books for children were made in those days, Ulysses was reading adult books when he was six years old. Mathematics was his strongest subject. He could blurt out answers to equations before most students even had the numbers written down. Ulysses' intelligence and horse-riding talents were clues that he was something special.

One day, a traveling **phrenologist** visited Georgetown. This man studied the shape of people's heads and then told them about their intelligence and character. He would describe what their future might be like. Many people thought that phrenologists were cheats. But Jesse wanted to hear about his son's future.

Rubbing the boy's head, the phrenologist acted excited. "It is an extraordinary head," he said. Jesse smiled. He knew his Ulysses was a special boy. "It would not be strange," the man continued, "if we should see him president of the United States!" No one, probably not even Jesse, could have imagined that.

The view from West Point, New York, was an impressive sight to Ulysses when he went to the military academy there. Ulysses worked hard and, by the time he graduated, made excellent grades.

"You Will Go!"

At age 17, Ulysses was nearing the end of his schooling. Only one of out every 100 young men went to college in those days. Jesse knew his son belonged in college, so he decided to enroll the teenager.

But Jesse didn't ask Ulysses what he wanted to do. Ulysses had just returned from his school in Ripley, Ohio, located about 10 miles away. He was home for Christmas break when Jesse said excitedly, "I believe you are going to receive the appointment!"

Jesse explained that because Ulysses wanted to

attend college, he had found a way for the boy to go for free. Through a congressman, Jesse had arranged for his boy to get a spot at West Point, the famous school for future soldiers.

"I won't go!" a shocked Ulysses protested. He never wanted to become a soldier, and that's exactly what West Point would make him: a military man.

"I think you will go," Jesse responded firmly, and that settled it. Jesse Grant had rarely ever ordered his son to do anything against his wishes. Yet the father knew what was good for his boy's future. He ordered Ulysses to attend the United States Military Academy at West Point.

In those days, only young men went to West Point. To be admitted, young men had to be in excellent health and ready for all the physical work of the military. Doctors would check them for sickness and injury. If they didn't pass the examination, they couldn't become a West Point student.

Four boys from Ulysses' neighborhood had successfully graduated from the military academy. But his next-door neighbor Bartlett Bailey was about to be kicked out for bad grades. Ulysses didn't want that embarrassment to happen to him. The determined young man would give it a try.

In May 1839, Ulysses boarded a steamboat in Ripley. Aboard the boat, a thought flashed through his mind. Maybe the steamboat would overheat and blow up. Then he would not have to go to the academy.

Ulysses was probably disappointed when the boat docked safely in Pittsburgh. From there, he traveled to Philadelphia and spent five days touring the city. Then he went to New York City and spent a few days visiting famous sights. The reluctant student would do anything to keep from arriving early at West Point.

Eventually, Ulysses boarded a boat heading north up the Hudson River. After traveling 80 miles, West Point came in to view. Located on a bluff high above the river, the academy overlooked all the surrounding country. It was a beautiful sight.

But Ulysses still wasn't happy. He was afraid of being teased, as he had been as a child back in Ohio. The initials for his full name–Hiram Ulysses Grant–spelled out the word "HUG." Somebody had even given him a trunk-size suitcase with his initials tacked onto it in brass. Ulysses had the letters removed, but he also had a plan to make sure no one at West Point ever learned what his initials spelled. He decided he would change his name by signing in as Ulysses Hiram Grant, or "UHG." Then no one would tease him.

Luckily for Ulysses, somebody had already changed his name for him. It seems that the congressman had mistakenly written his name as "Ulysses Simpson Grant" on the official form. Simpson was the maiden name of Ulysses' mother. The officers at West Point wouldn't let him change his name, so he became Ulysses

Ulysses' journey to West Point began on a steamboat like this one. His trip took many days, through Ohio, Pennsylvania, and New York.

Simpson Grant, or **Cadet U. S. Grant.**" The other cadets thought that "U. S." stood for United States or Uncle Sam. Most people started calling him "Sam."

Ulysses was one of about 100 young men

who were new to West Point. None of them were official students yet. Admittance required passing a **grueling** test. For two weeks, the young men lived in dark barracks on the outskirts of the academy. Doctors and officers poked and prodded their bodies, making sure they were healthy. The cadets drank well water and ate bad food. Only those who were fit and tough survived those weeks.

Then the young men who were declared physically fit sat down to take a long written exam about everything they had learned in school. The written test scared Ulysses. Though he had always been a decent student, he knew that his education hadn't been as good as that of many of these other young men. They came from rich families and had attended the best schools or had private **tutors**.

Although he had little hope of passing, Ulysses worked his way through the entrance exam. The young man hadn't enjoyed the past two weeks. He thought they were boring and tiring. But Ulysses had a funny feeling that West Point felt a little bit like home. It was a gut feeling that he couldn't explain or under-stand, but in a way, it felt as if he'd lived at West Point forever. Ulysses wanted to pass the test. And he did. On August 28, 1839, Ulysses S. Grant became an official West Point cadet.

Even then, things didn't get any easier. The cadets woke up every morning at 5 A.M. Their days were filled with school, military drills, and mushy food. Marching was particularly painful for Ulysses. He was tone-deaf and couldn't stand the beating drums. **Upperclassmen**, or older students, constantly picked on the newer cadets. The professors did little to stop this. It

Ulysses attended West Point with several young men who would become part of Civil War history. The most important were William Tecumseh Sherman, George McClellan, and Thomas Jackson. Sherman became famous as the Union general who torched a path through Georgia and the Carolinas. McClellan, a Northern general, ran for president against Abraham Lincoln in 1864. Jackson, a Southerner, became the Confederacy's famous "Stonewall" Jackson.

This portrait of Ulysses was made shortly after his graduation from West Point. At first he had trouble following the academy's strict rules, but Ulysses soon realized that his college degree would help him go far in life.

was a part of West Point preparation. If students could not handle their classmates' teasing, how would they deal with the stress of battle?

Unlike his childhood, Ulysses hardly got teased at all. However, he spent a lot of time in his room reading novels instead of doing his homework. The classes covered a wide variety of subjects, ranging from French to military tactics. The young cadet's favorite class was math. Ulysses never worked hard at becoming a top student. He usually ranked in the middle of his class.

The officers at West Point set strict rules for the cadets. Smoking and drinking were not allowed. Cadets had to be clean, respectful, and always on time. When a rule was broken, a cadet was given black marks, or **demerits**, and a stern punishment. Once, Ulysses was caught skipping church on a Sunday. He was assigned eight demerits and put under arrest. For a whole month, he could not leave his room other than to go to class.

If a cadet was charged with 200 or more demerits in a year, he would be kicked out of the academy. That never happened to Ulysses, but he was hardly perfect. Out of 223 cadets, he was ranked 156th in behavior.

During his second year at the academy, Ulysses became excited when he learned that Congress was thinking about closing West Point. He wanted to become a college mathematics professor, not a soldier. If Congress would shut down West Point, he could go to school somewhere else and be done with the military. But that hope soon faded.

As time passed, Ulysses slowly began to like the school for the same reasons his father had chosen it. If he worked hard enough to graduate, he would be able to do almost anything he wanted to do in life. Very few people could last long enough to graduate from West Point. Only 39 of the 100 candidates who joined Ulysses as freshmen graduated with him four years later.

By graduation, Ulysses was excelling at West Point. At the graduation ceremony in 1843, he set a school record for high jump atop a horse.

As the sergeant called out Ulysses' name, he streaked across the grounds and rode his horse to a perfect high leap of six feet. With that jump, Ulysses S. Grant became a graduate of West Point. Someday, he would become one of the academy's most famous graduates, but first he had to face many challenges.

Many thousands of infantry soldiers, such as these, practiced marching in formation for hours at a time. Ulysses wanted to be a cavalry officer but was assigned to the infantry instead.

The Brave Warrior

When he graduated from West Point, Ulysses became part of a special group of men. No longer was he "useless." No graduate of West Point was ever called that.

After graduation, Ulysses was required to join the army. The job he most wanted was as a member of the **cavalry**, the soldiers on horseback. With his riding skills, Ulysses would have gotten the job easily, but a mistake from the past haunted him.

In March of his final year at West Point, Ulysses had gotten angry with a horse. He pulled out his saber and struck the animal in rage. Ulysses was punished by having to stay in his room for two full weeks. But worse yet, his temper had cost him the cavalry job.

Instead, Ulysses was made an officer in the **infantry**. In the fall of 1843, Ulysses was stationed in Jefferson Barracks, located about 10 miles south of St. Louis, Missouri.

Ulysses' West Point roommate, Frederick T. Dent, was also stationed at Jefferson Barracks. The Dent family estate, White Haven, was located just five miles away from Jefferson Barracks. Colonel and Mrs. Dent, Fred's parents, often welcomed young officers, including Ulysses, into their cozy home.

Being so far away from his family in Ohio, Ulysses was lonely and enjoyed visiting the Dents. The young officer rode out to White Haven once or twice a week that winter, becoming close with the Dents and their daughters, 8-year-old Emma and 16-year-old Nellie.

Ulysses had heard about a third Dent girl,

When Ulysses was stationed in Missouri, he often visited the Dent family home, which was large and beautiful, like the house pictured here. There he met his future wife, Julia.

19-year-old Julia. She was Fred's favorite sister. Julia knew about Ulysses, too. Fred had told her about his roommate: a young, strong, master horseman.

Julia returned in the spring from her St.

Louis school, and Ulysses finally met her. The two instantly liked one another. Julia was about five feet tall, a couple of inches shorter than Ulysses, with thick black hair and sun-tanned skin. Ulysses began visiting more and more often, taking walks and horseback rides with Julia.

The two didn't talk about falling in love, but they were. Nellie and Emma noticed that Julia would take extra care to put ribbons in her hair and freshen up when she knew Ulysses would be visiting.

The young officer tried to do nice things for her, too. Julia had a pet canary that died. Ulysses made a small yellow coffin for the bird and held a funeral with eight soldiers. Ulysses began visiting at the Dents' home so much that he was often late for dinner back at Jefferson Barracks.

Meanwhile problems were growing between the United States and Mexico over land in Texas. War, it seemed, was coming. In April

1844, Ulysses left Jefferson Barracks for a three-week vacation back home. Just after he boarded a steamboat to Ohio, his **regiment** at Jefferson Barracks received orders to go to Louisiana. There they would prepare to fight against the Mexicans if a war broke out. Ulysses' leave was canceled, but he didn't find that out until a letter reached him in Ohio two weeks later.

The young man returned to Missouri immediately. After checking in at Jefferson Barracks, Ulysses rode through a flooding stream toward the Dents' estate. He wanted to say good-bye to Julia. But first, he had a big question for her.

Ulysses arrived dripping like a soaked rag doll, so he put off his question while changing into dry clothes. The Dents had to attend a family wedding in St. Louis the next day and asked Ulysses to come along. He agreed. The next day he and Julia rode alone in a buggy to the wedding.

When the horse stopped cautiously in front of a rickety bridge crossing over an overflowing stream, Julia was scared. "I'll take care of you," the young officer told Julia, a serious look on his face.

"I'm going to cling to you no matter what happens," she answered nervously.

Slowly and carefully, Ulysses guided the horse and buggy safely across the bridge. It took less than a minute. Once they were across, the couple smiled. For Ulysses, it was the perfect time to pop his question. Ulysses looked at Julia, asked, "How would you like to cling to me for the rest of your life?"

Julia realized that her brother's friend was asking her to marry him. She said yes. Over-joyed, the young man removed his West Point class ring, which he got when he graduated, and put it on Julia's finger as the symbol of their engagement.

Shortly afterward, Ulysses boarded a boat and headed to Louisiana to join his regiment. The men stayed there through the unbearably hot and humid summer. Then they were

In this drawing, American soldiers prepare for a battle during the war against Mexico. During the war, Ulysses fought bravely and was later honored for his courage in battle.

ordered to Corpus Christi, Texas.

Ulysses didn't like going to war against Mexico, but it wasn't his choice. If ordered to fight, he would follow the order and do his duty well.

In 1836, Texas declared itself independent from Mexico. Sam Houston, the leader of Texas, asked the United States to **annex** his country, and Texas became a state in 1845.

Meanwhile, the United States was claiming 150 miles of land between the Rio Grande and the Neuces River. Mexico insisted it owned this land, but the United States wouldn't give it up. What followed was the Mexican War.

When the order finally arrived, Ulysses performed bravely. In a battle at the Mexican city of Monterrey, Ulysses' troops ran out of ammunition. Someone was needed to cross through enemy fire, get to the U.S. army command base, and request help.

"It's a very dangerous job and I don't like to order any man to do it," said Lieutenant Colonel John Garland. "Who'll volunteer?"

Ulysses stepped forward. "I will! I've got a horse!" He wrapped his hands in the horse's mane, put one foot underneath the saddle, and rode away. Riding on the side of the horse, Ulysses was shielded from a shower of bullets.

"There goes a man of fire!" Garland cried.

Ulysses was also caring and creative in battles.

At Vera Cruz, he saw Fred Dent had been shot in the leg. Risking his own life, Ulysses ran up to Fred and pulled him to safety. While Ulysses was saving Fred, a Mexican tried to kill him, but another U.S. soldier shot the Mexican and saved both Ulysses and Fred.

In Mexico City, Ulysses and another soldier came upon a church and convinced the priest to let them inside. Ulysses brought a **howitzer** —a small cannon—into the bell tower. They used it to shoot down incoming enemies. After the war ended with an American victory in 1848, Ulysses was honored for his bravery.

Ulysses married Julia Dent (shown here) in 1848. They wanted to spend time together as a family, but Ulysses was often stationed far away, sometimes in places where it was not safe for Julia to visit him.

Hard, Scrambling Years

Throughout the Mexican War, Ulysses had been thinking about his fiancée, Julia. Every time he wrote her a letter, which was often, he kissed it before sending it on its way. The smitten young man missed her so badly that he pulled a tuft of chin hairs from his beard and mailed them to Julia as a way to remember him. Julia mailed Ulysses some pressed flower petals, but they blew away in the wind when he opened the letter before he noticed them.

While Ulysses spent time battling against the Mexicans and becoming a war hero, Julia was living in St. Louis. During the day she attended school. Nighttime brought parties and other social events. Julia's father, Colonel Dent, was hoping that she would break off her engagement to Ulysses and find a rich Southern boy to marry instead, but she remained faithful to her love.

Ulysses and Julia were married on August 22, 1848, inside a small house in St. Louis. Ulysses' parents didn't attend. As Northerners, they didn't like Ulysses marrying the daughter of a Southern slave owner. Ulysses didn't like slavery, either, but he loved Julia. With peace at hand in the United States, Ulysses was sent to Sackets Harbor, New York, and then to Detroit, Michigan. Julia traveled right by his side.

The couple remained together until Julia became pregnant in 1849. Wanting to be around her mother and sisters while raising a baby, Julia returned to St. Louis without her husband. In June 1850 she gave birth to Frederick Dent Grant. Ulysses called their first child "the little dog" and loved to get letters about his son. Julia and baby

Fred joined him from time to time as the regiment moved between Sackets Harbor and Detroit.

Two years later, Ulysses learned that his regiment would be moving to northern California. He insisted that Fred and Julia, who was pregnant again, stay at home with her parents. The trip to California was difficult and dangerous in those days. Most people traveled to the West Coast by taking a ship from an East Coast port and sailing south on the Atlantic Ocean to the nation of Panama. The Panama Canal had not been built, so travelers crossed though the jungle on mules and then took another ship north on the Pacific Ocean.

Leaving his family at home was a wise choice. Ulysses was put in charge of helping the soldiers' families (about 60 women and 20 children) cross the **isthmus** of Panama. Many people died, mostly from the disease **cholera**. This illness was spread in two ways. Sometimes flies landed on the waste of sick people and then carried germs to healthy people's food. Other times, healthy people drank spring water that had been polluted by the bodies and waste of sick people.

Ulysses turned a broken-down ship on the beach into a cholera hospital. He attended to the sick people with care and love, but he couldn't work miracles. He could never forget the many people who died in front of him.

Eventually Ulysses arrived in San Francisco. His ship wasn't alone. This was the time of the famous California Gold Rush. People were moving in daily, hoping to cash in on their dreams of finding gold and becoming rich. Most of the 50,000 people living in San Francisco believed in taking risks. They were willing to take big chances in order to fulfill their dreams.

Ulysses' dream was to have his growing family join him. He missed them terribly. The young father hadn't even seen his second child, Ulysses Jr., who had been named for him. Ulysses turned to drinking alcohol so he could forget his problems. Sometimes he drank so much that he lost control of his actions and got himself into trouble.

For Julia to be able to come to California, Ulysses would have to save enough money to pay for her trip and hire a servant. The young army officer invested some of his money to help a friend open a store in Fort Vancouver, located in what is now Washington State. Ulysses also set up a potato-selling business. Finally, he saved enough money to have Julia and their two children come out to the West Coast. But they never did.

Ulysses grew more depressed. He kept drinking. Although he was a likable man who loved telling Mexican War stories, his army **peers** began to lose trust in him when they saw him drunk. One of those officers was George McClellan, a West Point classmate.

Meanwhile, Ulysses' businesses were going bad. The price of potatoes dropped, so he lost a lot of money in his crop business. He tried to open a hotel with some army friends, but that didn't work out either.

Ulysses was broke and depressed. More than

anything, he missed his family. So on April 11, 1854, just after being promoted to army captain, he wrote a letter of resignation. When Jesse Grant found out that his son had quit the army, he was **livid**.

Ulysses returned home to St. Louis, but his two children didn't even know who he was. Four-year-old Fred and two-year-old Ulysses were scared of the stranger when they first saw him. Then a slave told them that the man was their father.

Ulysses wanted his family to have their own home, so he spent two years building a log cabin in St. Louis. When the simple, white house was finished, he called it "Hardscrabble." Not nearly as luxurious as Colonel Dent's estate, Hardscrabble had only what was needed: three bedrooms, two floors, and a roof.

Julia didn't like her new home, but she did not have to live there long. Three months after the Grants moved into Hardscrabble, Julia's mother died. The family moved back to White

After Ulysses left the army he tried farming and several other businesses. Unfortunately he lost money again and again.

Haven to look after Colonel Dent.

Ulysses enjoyed being with his family. By 1858, Julia had given birth to two more babies, Nellie and Jesse. These children ended up being the youngest in the family.

Ulysses was close to all four of his children: Frederick, Ulysses Jr. (nicknamed "Buck"), Ellen (called "Nellie"), and Jesse. When he was home, Ulysses loved to read stories aloud to the family at night. This was their favorite form of entertainment.

Fred went on to college at West Point. Buck became a student at Harvard. Nellie, who lived in the White House while her father was president, married an Englishman and moved to England. Jesse, the youngest, wrote a book about living in the White House.

But these were also difficult years. Living with Colonel Dent was torture because the old man and Ulysses simply didn't get along. Earning money was getting more difficult, too. Ulysses had been farming and selling firewood, but American business hit hard times in 1857. The former army captain lost most of his money.

Driven out of business, Ulysses took a job as a rent collector. He worked for Julia's cousin, Harry Boggs, collecting money from people whose bills were overdue. But Ulysses was not good at the job. He had a big heart and couldn't bear to force people to pay money they didn't have.

Other job offers came along. But being

superintendent of roads and customs officer didn't work either. Finally Ulysses moved his family to Galena, Illinois, where his brothers Orvil and Simpson ran a leather store. There Ulysses worked as a clerk, but not for long.

Trouble was brewing between the North and the South. The argument was about slavery and the rights of states to make their own laws. A battle was about to break out. The fight would one day be known as the Civil War.

Ulysses helped recruit soldiers for the Union army at a recruiting center like the one pictured here. But he still had trouble becoming an officer because he hadn't been in the army for several years.

A War Within the Family

Ulysses knew about fighting within a family. Julia's father was a slave owner. Ulysses hated slavery and didn't like Colonel Dent much, either.

At the same time, something was happening between the **free states** of the North and the **slave states** of the South. A war within the country was about to break out. The **Union**, as the North was called, needed bigger armed forces.

Once the Civil War began in April 1861, President Lincoln asked state governors to set up volunteer **militias**. Ulysses desperately wanted to become a colonel and run a regiment. He volunteered to do paperwork and help register the soldiers in Illinois, hoping it would lead to his appointment as a colonel in charge of a regiment. It didn't.

Frustrated and disappointed, Ulysses traveled to Cincinnati, Ohio, where George McClellan was in charge of setting up regiments. But when Ulysses got there, McClellan wouldn't see him.

Ulysses heard that Illinois governor Richard Yates was searching for someone to control the Seventh District Regiment. The men were causing trouble and refused to obey their commanders. Many of the men knew Ulysses because he had helped recruit them weeks earlier. They asked for Captain Grant to be put in charge.

Governor Yates didn't like the idea because Ulysses had quit the army seven years earlier. But he needed somebody who could control the regiment, so he asked Ulysses to take the job. Ulysses quickly accepted.

Ulysses' 600 men were farmers. None of them had military training. Their new leader decided to train them himself.

His first lesson was to teach his men that military rules needed to be followed. If an individual or group of soldiers broke rules, they were punished. Ulysses' men quickly learned that he was a serious boss.

Finally the time came for Ulysses' troops to move into battle. His regiment first marched toward Confederate colonel Thomas Harris in northern Missouri. Ulysses was nervous. Then his troops came to a point where they had a full view of the valley below. Colonel Harris's men were gone. They had fled when they heard that Union troops were coming. Ulysses suddenly realized that the Confederates were just as scared of him as he was of them. Never again was he afraid of moving toward the enemy.

As he proved his ability to lead men into battle, Ulysses' army grew. His first great victory came in northern Tennessee during February 1862. With 15,000 men under his command, Ulysses moved toward Fort Henry on the Tennessee

River. He had six times as many men as the Confederates had stationed at Fort Henry. Even in cold, pouring rain, Ulysses took the fort easily.

But the job was not finished yet. Around 2,500 Southern soldiers from Fort Henry had been sent to Fort Donelson, located about 12 miles away. Moving east, Ulysses' troops advanced on Fort Donelson by foot. They were supported by seven gunboats.

The heavy rain that had poured on Fort Henry had turned to snow and sleet. It was February 13, 1862, an unlucky day for the **Confederacy**. Surrounded by troops and armed boats for two days, the Southerners attempted to break out of the fort.

At first, it looked like the Confederates might

During the Civil War, children sometimes helped out at camps by washing clothes, helping cook food, or running errands for soldiers. At Vicksburg, Ulysses was soaking his dentures in a washbowl. A young girl, trying to be helpful, emptied the washbowl into the river. She did not know the false teeth were inside. No one could get them back. Ulysses had to eat soft food for a few days until a dentist arrived to make a new set of teeth for him.

actually break free, but soon they retreated back inside under a shower of bullets from the Union troops. Inside, the Confederate leaders discussed what to do. One of them was General Simon B. Buckner, an old friend of Ulysses'. He asked the Union general if they could work out a deal for surrender.

Ulysses sent a note back, saying, "No terms except unconditional and immediate surrender can be accepted." With no other choice, the Confederates surrendered on February 16. That was the day U. S. Grant earned a new nickname: "Unconditional Surrender."

Ulysses was a **relentless** warrior. His bloodiest battle happened just two months later on the grounds surrounding the Shiloh Church in Tennessee. The Confederates had surprised the 40,000 troops in the Federal Army of the Tennessee. But Ulysses refused to surrender and kept his troops fighting. In the meantime, the 25,000-man Army of the Ohio quietly arrived, giving the Northerners more strength.

On the next morning, the Confederate leaders thought they'd won the battle. They didn't know the Ohio troops had arrived. Using that element of surprise, the Union forces drubbed the Confederates, who surrendered.

Twenty-three thousand soldiers were killed, wounded, or captured that day, but the North won the battle. Some people called Ulysses a "butcher," but President Lincoln was proud of his warrior. "I cannot spare this man," the president said. "He fights."

For Ulysses, war was a test of willpower. The side that gave in first would be the loser. The side that held its strength no matter what happened would win. This was how Ulysses Grant won the famous Vicksburg Campaign. During that campaign, he spent nine months fighting a battle of wills with the Confederacy.

A heavily guarded Confederate fort, Vicksburg stood high on a bluff above the Mississippi River. It was from there that the Confederates sent their weapons and supplies down the river to their other

Ulysses (behind the flag and cannon) urges his men on in battle. The Battle of Shiloh, in April 1862, was the first battle in North America in which 100,000 troops fought.

bases and encampments. The Union troops knew if they could seize Vicksburg, the Southern soldiers' supplies would be cut off. That would be a big step toward claiming Union victory in the war. Ulysses decided to take the fort.

Since the summer of 1862, Union soldiers had been trying to penetrate Vicksburg with no luck. Ulysses figured that it would take a lot of time and patience. In April 1863, he began moving his men into the state of Mississippi and toward its capital, Jackson. He knew that if his troops took Jackson, the Confederates would not have enough strength to defend Vicksburg.

He was right. The Union forces overtook Jackson and began focusing on Vicksburg. Taking that guarded city, however, was a tougher assignment. Ulysses' troops were able to trap the Confederates inside Vicksburg, but they weren't strong enough to rush inside and seize the city in one triumphant attack. Instead, Union troops camped outside Vicksburg and stayed there for 47 days.

For those 47 days, no food or weapons entered Vicksburg. None got to the Union troops either. Both sides were living off the land. They found food and shelter in any way possible. The men ate the meat of horses, dogs, cats, and rats. Survival was the goal. If the Union troops turned around and left, the Confederacy would win the battle. Despite the cries of many of his men, Ulysses would not retreat. He had always felt superstitious about retracing his steps.

Finally, on July 4, the 47th day of the **siege**, the Confederates sent a flag of surrender, giving up Vicksburg to the North. Shortly after Ulysses' victory, President Lincoln named him lieutenant general of all United States armies.

Many people thought that the siege of Vicksburg would win the war for the North, but it wasn't that simple. For two more years, battles raged on. Ulysses and his troops played a big role in a major victory at Chattanooga in September 1863. They spent many weeks pursuing Southern general Robert E. Lee and his troops.

They caught up to Lee in April 1865, when Union forces took control of the Confederate capital, Richmond, Virginia. General Lee, knowing the war was lost for the South, said, "There is nothing left me but to go and see General Grant, and I had rather die a thousand deaths."

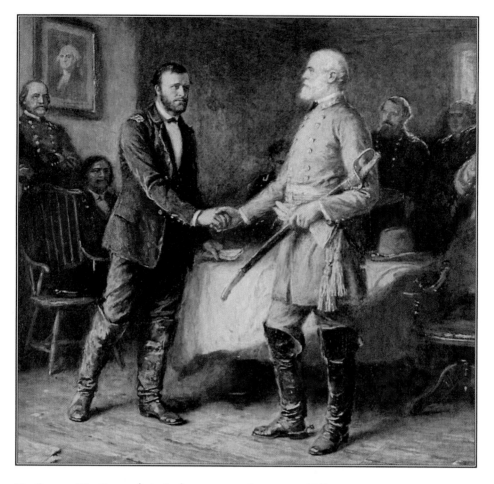

Robert E. Lee (right) surrenders to Ulysses at Appomattox Court House, Virginia. Their meeting marked the end of the Civil War.

On April 9, at around one o'clock in the afternoon, General Lee, dressed in his finest uniform, arrived at Appomattox Courthouse. He was there to surrender to the North.

Ulysses arrived a half hour later, dressed in muddy clothing. He was about to make peace with the same people he had been hunting for four years. Despite his dirty uniform, Ulysses wanted to make peace like a gentleman. He tried to make small talk about the Mexican War, hoping it would make everyone less nervous, but that didn't work.

So the two generals got down to business. Ulysses simply wanted the Southerners to return to their homes. He would give them food for the trip and allow them to keep their horses for the ride. Ulysses promised that the Southern soldiers would be treated well as long as they obeyed the law.

General Lee offered his sword as a symbol of the South's surrender, but Ulysses refused to take it. Though Lee was older, both men had graduated from West Point. They had once fought in the Mexican War for the same country, the United States. Now they were united again. Ulysses wanted Lee and everyone else to know that it was time for peace.

Ulysses posed for this portrait in his army uniform. After the Civil War ended, he became famous and successfully ran for the presidency.

"Let Us Have Peace"

After the Civil War ended, Ulysses became a national hero—to most people, at least. The first time he visited his mother, Hannah, she looked at him and said, "Well, Ulysses, you've become quite a great man, haven't you?" Then she continued to do her household chores.

Ulysses was a lot like his mother. He was not easily impressed and didn't like to make small talk. So it was quite a surprise when the Republican Party offered him the nomination for the presidency in 1868.

At the time, Ulysses was secretary of war under President Andrew Johnson. He had been named a full general by Congress. (The last person to hold that title was George Washington.) Ulysses was one of history's greatest soldiers, but he was unsure about being president. Not only did he not like politics, but he had only voted for a president once in his entire life. Still, he was honored. At the end of his letter accepting the nomination, Ulysses asked for peace.

Ulysses won the election easily and was sworn into office in March 1869. His big goal was to reduce the national debt and get rid of war taxes. Ulysses wanted to be known as a president who got the country's finances in order and kept the peace. But that wouldn't happen.

The presidency did not suit Ulysses. A good president must be able to pick honest, hard-working people to serve in his **cabinet** and on his staff. When Ulysses submitted his list of choices for cabinet members to Congress, the Republicans were shocked. The president had never asked for their help in choosing the men for these important jobs, and many of the people

Ulysses picked were crooks who cheated, lied, and stole from the government. The president even had problems with a dishonest brother-in-law who stole $11 million from the country's gold reserves.

Ulysses should have asked more people to help him pick his cabinet. For the next eight years, the Grant administration was full of scandals. Different problems came up with tax collections. The attorney general and federal judges also turned out to be untrustworthy. These were people who were supposed to **enforce** the law.

Several more cabinet secretaries also had problems. Ulysses' first vice president, Schuyler Colfax, was accused of stealing money from the Transcontinental Railroad. Colfax was not asked to serve for the second term.

Nobody ever thought Ulysses was a liar, but most people blamed him for doing a bad job when he picked the people who worked for him. Still, Americans remembered him as a war hero and reelected him as president in 1872.

Though he felt a duty to serve the country,

Ulysses never enjoyed being president. Julia, on the other hand, loved living in the White House. She held lots of fancy parties and dinners. Ulysses didn't like these social events, but he loved being with Julia, so he went along with her ideas. Besides, he had to be there. Everyone wanted to meet President Grant.

Julia had a trick to get her husband to talk to other people. She would begin to tell a story, but include a wrong detail on purpose. Ulysses would interrupt and correct her, then finish the story. Once Ulysses refused to see a man who had made an appointment. When Julia found out about it, she sent her husband a note. "Dear Ulyss– Do please make this appointment. Julia." Right away, Ulysses saw the man.

Nellie and Jesse, the two younger children, loved living in the White House almost as much as their mother did. Jesse called the White House "the best playground in the world." He had a big telescope on the roof of the White House. With his father, Jesse would sometimes stay out late at night,

Ulysses' children Nellie and Frederick Grant (shown here) loved living in the White House while their father was president.

stargazing until Julia would call them in to bed.

When Jesse had a problem, he sometimes asked his father's cabinet for a solution. And they did give him answers. Jesse also had many pet dogs, but they always seemed to die. Eventually President Grant called a meeting of the White House staff. He claimed that everyone would be fired if any more of Jesse's dogs died. No more dogs died.

As for Nellie, it seemed that all of America loved this pretty teenager. She was often referred to as a "princess." She traveled to England in 1872. When she returned to her family, she was in love. Soon she became engaged to a young man named Algernon Sartoris.

Their wedding was set for May 21, 1874, and it was one of the most elaborate marriage ceremonies ever held in the White House. Several hundred people gathered in the East Room, which was decorated with orange blossoms and roses. The guests feasted on several varieties of meat, crab, and delicious cake.

The festivities were grand, but Ulysses was sad. After Nellie left that night, the president was found crying in her room.

This was the sensitive side of Ulysses. For a warrior who fought foes to the death, he had a soft side. Ulysses disliked dirty jokes and hated swearing. Animal lover that he was, he wouldn't eat meat.

One day, Ulysses was driving his horse and buggy down M Street in Washington when an officer pulled him over. The buggy was traveling too fast, and the policeman was about to issue a speeding ticket. Suddenly he noticed that the driver was the president. The officer was going to let him go free, but Ulysses wouldn't allow it.

"Officer, do your duty," he said. So President Grant received a speeding ticket and walked home to the White House.

When Ulysses' second term ended, he and Julia took their time walking through the White House on their last day. Looking around the building one last time brought back memories. The Grants had lived in the White House longer than anywhere else in their lives, and they hated to leave. Though being president is a difficult job, living in the White House was a pleasure.

Soon after leaving the White House, Ulysses, Julia, and 19-year-old Jesse took a two-year vacation around the world. In both Europe and

Asia they were greeted by kings, queens, and prime ministers. Ulysses was a huge celebrity and was treated like royalty everywhere he went.

In 1880, the Grants were back in the United States. Ulysses needed a job. He'd been president before, but this time, he didn't get the nomination. There would be no third term for President Grant.

That was disappointing, but things soon became even worse. Ulysses invested his life savings in a financial company that his son Buck was starting with a man named Ferdinand Ward. Ward, however, turned out to be a con artist. Within three years, all the former president's money was lost.

Then one day, while munching on some fruit, Ulysses felt a sharp pain sting his throat. Smoking nearly two dozen cigars a day had finally caught up with him. He had throat cancer and would probably die within a few months. His only wish was to find a way to make some money for his family before he died.

His wish came true when he met Mark Twain. The man who would one day become famous for writing about Tom Sawyer and Huckleberry Finn was introduced to Ulysses. Twain offered to publish an **autobiography** if Ulysses would write it.

This seemed the only way to earn some money so that Julia could live comfortably after Ulysses was gone. In the spring of 1885, the dying man began writing furiously. Racing against cancer to provide for his family would be the last battle of his life. He became so sick that he could barely talk, but he kept writing.

Ulysses and Julia are both buried in Grant's Tomb, a national monument located on the island of Manhattan in New York City. Visitors can see a museum of Grant's life and the side-by-side tombs of the couple, as well as visit the gift shop. Built over 100 years ago, the tomb was refurbished in the 1990s. It is open year-round.

In July, Ulysses finished writing his **memoirs**. Just a few days later, on July 23, he died. *Personal Memoirs* became a bestseller, earning nearly

Grant's Tomb, located in New York City, is the final resting place of both Ulysses and his wife.

$450,000 for Julia and their family. He didn't live to see it, but Ulysses S. Grant won the final fight of his life.

GLOSSARY

annex–to make part of something larger, as when a country adds another state

autobiography–a book in which a person tells the story of his or her own life

cabinet–the group of advisers who work with the president

cadet–a soldier in training

cavalry–a group of soldiers who ride horses

cholera–a deadly disease affecting the stomach and intestines

Confederacy–the group of Southern states that fought against the Union during the Civil War

demerits–marks against one's record which can lead to punishment

enforce–to make sure something, such as laws, are obeyed

free states–states in which slavery was not allowed

grueling–difficult and tiring

hides–the skins of dead animals

howitzer–a short cannon

infantry–a group of soldiers who travel on foot

isthmus–a narrow strip of land that connects two larger pieces of land

livery–a stable where people are paid to care for horses

livid–very angry

memoirs–an autobiography

militia–an army of citizens who are not regular soldiers

peers–people who share the same standing because of age, grade, or status

phrenologist–a person who studied the shape of other people's heads to predict their intelligence and character

regiment–a large military unit made up of many smaller groups

relentless–showing no sign of giving up or becoming weaker

siege–a blockade around a city or fort to force it to surrender

slave states–states in which slavery was legal

tannery–a shop where leather was made

tannic acid–a substance made from oak bark that is used in tanning leather

tutors–private teachers

Union–the group of states that fought against the Confederacy during the Civil War

upperclassmen–members of the two highest grades in high school and college

CHRONOLOGY

1822	Born in Point Pleasant, Ohio, on April 27.
1823	Family moves to Georgetown, Ohio.
1839	Begins training at the United States Military Academy at West Point.
1843	Graduates from West Point and begins army career in Jefferson Barracks, Missouri.
1845–48	Fights in the Mexican War and earns honors.
1848	Marries Julia Dent on August 22.
1854	Resigns from the army and returns to Missouri.
1861	Volunteers to help the Union army in the war against the South; is made a brigadier general.
1862	Attacks and captures Fort Henry and Fort Donelson in February.
1863	Takes Vicksburg on July 4.
1864	Named lieutenant general of all U.S. armies by President Lincoln.
1865	Accepts Confederate general Robert E. Lee's unconditional surrender on April 9 at the Appomattox Court House.
1868	Elected to the presidency.
1872	Reelected to the presidency for a second term.

1877   Leaves the White House; takes a vacation around the world.

1884   Learns he has throat cancer; begins writing his memoirs.

1885   Finishes his autobiography in July; dies on July 23 in Mount McGregor, New York.

CIVIL WAR TIME LINE ====

1860   Abraham Lincoln is elected president of the United States on November 6. During the next few months, Southern states begin to break away from the Union.

1861   On April 12, the Confederates attack Fort Sumter, South Carolina, and the Civil War begins. Union forces are defeated in Virginia at the First Battle of Bull Run (First Manassas) on July 21 and withdraw to Washington, D.C.

1862   Robert E. Lee is placed in command of the main Confederate army in Virginia in June. Lee defeats the Army of the Potomac at the Second Battle of Bull Run (Second Manassas) in Virginia on August 29–30. On September 17, Union general George B. McClellan turns back Lee's first invasion of the North at Antietam Creek near Sharpsburg, Maryland. It is the bloodiest day of the war.

1863   On January 1, President Lincoln issues the Emancipation Proclamation, freeing slaves in Southern states. Between May 1–6, Lee wins an important victory at Chancellorsville, but key Southern commander Thomas J. "Stonewall" Jackson dies from wounds. In June, Union forces hold the city of Vicksburg, Mississippi, under siege. The people of Vicksburg surrender on July 4. Lee's second invasion of the North during July 1–3 is decisively turned back at Gettysburg, Pennsylvania.

1864 General Grant is made supreme Union commander on March 9. Following a series of costly battles, on June 19 Grant successfully encircles Lee's troops in Petersburg, Virginia. A siege of the town lasts nearly a year. Union general William Sherman captures Atlanta on September 2 and begins the "March to the Sea," a campaign of destruction across Georgia and South Carolina. On November 8, Abraham Lincoln wins reelection as president.

1865 On April 2, Petersburg, Virginia, falls to the Union. Lee attempts to reach Confederate forces in North Carolina but is gradually surrounded by Union troops. Lee surrenders to Grant on April 9 at Appomattox, Virginia, ending the war. Abraham Lincoln is assassinated by John Wilkes Booth on April 14.

FURTHER READING

Archer, Jules. *A House Divided: The Lives of Ulysses S. Grant and Robert E. Lee.* New York: Scholastic, 1997.

Moore, Kay. *. . . If You Lived at the Time of the Civil War.* New York: Scholastic, 1994.

Sandler, Martin W. *Civil War: A Library of Congress Book.* New York: HarperCollins Publishers, 1996.

Savage, Douglas J. *The Soldier's Life in the Civil War.* Philadelphia: Chelsea House Publishers, 2000.

Wroble, Lisa A. *Kids During the American Civil War.* New York: The Rosen Publishing Group, 1997.

INDEX

PICTURE CREDITS

ABOUT THE AUTHOR

A professional writer since the age of 16, **TIM O'SHEI** has covered the NHL and NFL for several national magazines. He has written three sports books for children and contributed to adult sports books. Tim enjoys history and has interviewed Presidents Gerald Ford and Jimmy Carter. He was assisted on this book by six future authors: Caitlin Durkin, Erin McKenna, Michelle McNamara, Katie Podyma, Jessica Raniero, and Chris Weber.

Senior Consulting Editor **ARTHUR M. SCHLESINGER, JR.** is the leading American historian of our time. He won the Pulitzer Prize for his book *The Age of Jackson* (1945), and again for *A Thousand Days* (1965). This chronicle of the Kennedy Administration also won a National Book Award. He has written many other books, including a multi-volume series, *The Age of Roosevelt.* Professor Schlesinger is the Albert Schweitzer Professor of the Humanities at the City University of New York, and has been involved in several other Chelsea House projects, including the COLONIAL LEADERS series of biographies on the most prominent figures of early American history.

jB
GRANT   O'Shei, Tim.

          Ulysses S. Grant.

$20.85

DATE			

DEC 4 2001

BAKER & TAYLOR